You Said You Missed My Poetry

Ragan Oliver

BookLeaf
Publishing

India | USA | UK

Presentation by *BookLeaf Publishing*

Web: www.bookleafpub.com

E-mail: info@bookleafpub.com

ISBN: 9789363313811

First edition 2024

To Ciera,

Love of my life

CiSah

Beautiful

Babe

You are worth every word.

And so much more.

ACKNOWLEDGEMENT

Match Group, Inc.
Waffle House #2213
Shelby Farms Park

PREFACE

I started writing the night we met.
Telling our story on paper was the only way
that I knew to make sure it was real.
To make sure you were real.

I started writing you poems the day we started
dating.
Hopefully to find a way to explain
what I knew was real.

And daily,
I am still surprised.
Surprised by you.
Surprised by your love.

12.2.23

Yesterday, you said

"ASK AGAIN"

with more romance.

It took me an entire day for me to figure out
how to breathe with that question on my mind.

Today, you said

"Yes"

and it stole my breath.

And the air escaped
from my lungs again.

but now
I never want to learn to breathe

properly

if it means
breathing without

you.

12.3.23

You asked if I was sick of being around you yet

I've been sick to my stomach all day

Only because I know that when tomorrow comes

I won't be around you anymore

12.4.23

Returning to
"real life"
isn't life at all

when all I want is
A REAL LIFE
with you.

12.5.23

I started looking at rings today.
How absolutely ridiculous is that?
I've known you for a little over a week.
But I'm completely sure that you're the one.

I started looking at rings today.
How absolutely ridiculous is that?
I don't want to wake up another day
without you in my life.

I started looking at rings today.
How absolutely ridiculous is that?
I never wanted to get married again.

How absolutely ridiculous is that?

I started looking at rings today.

12.8.23

Sometimes things are shorter than they should
be.

Sometimes they are longer than the best dream.

I hope for the latter but know its the first.

Because there's nowhere near enough life on this
earth

for me to ever get enough of you.

12.9.23

You haven't said 'I love you' yet.
I know that you want to.
It doesn't matter to me.
Because the way that you hold my hand
and the way that you breathe when we kiss
tells me everything that your words can't say.
You haven't said 'I love you' yet.
So I'll say it enough for the both of us.

12.13.23

I want to love you so well
that should there be anyone after me
they will come to know my heart
to understand your soul.

I want to leave an imprint on
your heart so deep that they
feel me in the space between
your fingers.

12.15.23

I never fully understood "I must have loved you
in a thousand lifetimes" until your fingers
interlaced in mine. And when you fit perfectly in
my arms, I knew we fit too well to not have
done this at least a thousand times before.

12.16.23

I would rather drown
trying to navigate the
storms of your contention
than sleep safely on the
shore never having
experienced the waves
of your love.

12.20.23

It was fall, almost winter, but the warmth of your
smile could have fooled me into believing that
you had brought the beach with you.
You talked of your trauma in jest, a story told
too many times to many undeserving assholes
who never valued the complexity and plot
enough, and I ate every word, swallowed it
whole-

smothered, covered, and diced,

with a side of jalapeños,
the perfect spice to my neurodivergence, the
creamer in your burnt coffee,
the painted-on eyebrows that had you ready to
fight
within 30 minutes of knowing me
because she smiled just a little too long.

You were wild.

Untamed.

Unhinged.

But I was the one who took you into the woods
on our first date.
I was the one who introduced you to my son
within 15 hours of meeting you.
I was the one who knew 8 minutes into texting
you that my life was never going to be the same.

I was insane.

And I never believed in love at first sight.
But I'm now a firm believer in love at first
swipe.
smothered, covered, and diced.

12.26.23

I look at you and I no longer see a woman.

I no longer see a human.

I see art.

Poetry.

A sculpture.

A painting.

A song.

The hum of which will go on forever.

Even after your hands have left mine.

1.12.24

There's an entire universe between your thighs.
I am an intrepid explorer
eager to mark off every new land and territory as
my own.
Knowing I will never fully understand
the depth and magnitude of your uncharted
wealth,
but hopeful and excited nonetheless.

1.14.24

It's a celebration of your birth today.

How selfish is it that I am the one receiving the gift?

2.2.24

The stars are jealous of how much light you
bring into this world.

For even they have to wait for their time to
shimmer in the sky.

But even on your hardest days,

you shine brighter than the sun.

2.14.24

I told you I've always hated Valentine's Day.

You apologized.

I thought that was a weird response.

Until I felt your love on February 14th

and realized it was no different than every other
day with you.

And then I understood

how amazing Valentine's Day is

when you are truly loved.

3.4.24

Poe lied when he said nevermore.

Because in all of the immortality

of his legacy,

he never knew

the eternity

of your love.

Your love is

Evermore.

4.1.24

I watch your chest rise and fall with each breath you take, and I can't help but be jealous of the air that gets to dance within your bloodstream. To encapsulate your lungs and feel your warmth as the sound of your heartbeat serenades me to sleep is all I could ever hope and dream.

I watch your eyes flutter underneath your eyelids in your sleep, and I can't help but be jealous of the darkness behind those eyelashes, embracing gently the vale brown and green that felt like the home we dream of deep within the forests of a far away land we've never seen.

I watch your fingers dance as you act out the dreams in your head, and I can't help but be jealous of the space between those fingers-- a space I long to occupy every moment of every day.

I am jealous of the sun because when daylight comes, it will steal you away.

I am jealous of the moon because she dances with you while my body sleeps.

I am jealous of space

and time

and matter

and anything

that keeps me away from you.

4.6.24

I knew.
I knew long before today that I was going to
marry you.
I knew 8 minutes into texting that I wanted to
know you.
I knew the minute our bodies collided that I
needed more of you.
I knew 20 minutes into talking that I was never
going to grow tired of you.
I knew a week into knowing you that my heart
could never let go of you.
I knew a month into dating you when I wanted
to propose to you.
I knew long before today that I wanted you.

But today you took my niece to get ice cream.
After you worked the face painting booth at my
kid's birthday party.

And today you reminded me that I'm going to
marry you.

4.22.24

I came to you with a thousand broken pieces

and you showed me the true art of stained glass windows

when you loved me back and made me whole.

6.2.24

I fell deeply in love with the way that the moon danced across your cheeks as if it had been searching the entire night for you.

I fell madly in love with the way that the earth seemed to paint you in the forest hues, reminding me of the home I thought I could never earn.

I fell madly in love with the way that the fire highlighted your eyes, the embers of your passion and desire.

I fell madly in love with the way that the air felt light and crisp when you came around, lifting the weight of the tragedy I had found.

I fell madly in love with the way that the water wrapped itself around your legs, showing me how to hold you the way you deserved.

I fell madly in love with the way that the Sun highlighted your eyes as if it had waited eons for your return.

Today

Ciera,
Will
    You
Marry
    Me?

www.ingramcontent.com/pod-product-compliance
Lightning Source LLC
Chambersburg PA
CBHW071245140726
47996CB00007B/2761